A Note to Parents and Teachers

Dorling Kindersley Readers is a compelling new reading programme for children, designed in conjunction with leading literacy experts, including Cliff Moon M.Ed., Honorary Fellow of the University of Reading. Cliff Moon has spent many years as a teacher and teacher educator specializing in reading and has written more than 140 books for children and teachers. He reviews regularly for teachers' journals.

Beautiful illustrations and superb full-colour photographs combine with engaging, easy-to-read stories to offer a fresh approach to each subject in the series. Each *Dorling Kindersley Reader* is guaranteed to capture a child's interest while developing his or her reading skills, general knowledge, and love of reading.

The four levels of *Dorling Kindersley Readers* are aimed at different reading abilities, enabling you to choose the books that are exactly right for your child:

Level 1 – Beginning to read
Level 2 – Beginning to read alone
Level 3 – Reading alone
Level 4 – Proficient readers

The "normal" age at which a child begins to read can be anywhere from three to eight years old, so these levels are intended only as a general guideline.

No matter which level you select, you can be sure that you are helping children learn to read, then read to learn!

D1425082

Dorling **DK** Kindersley

LONDON, NEW YORK, SYDNEY, DELHI, PARIS,
MUNICH and JOHANNESBURG

Project Editors Naia Bray-Moffatt,
Deborah Murrell
Art Editor Jane Horne
Senior Art Editor Sarah Ponder
Managing Editor Bridget Gibbs
Senior DTP Designer Bridget Roseberry
Production Melanie Dowland
Picture Researcher Frances Vargo
Jacket Designer Dean Price
Indexer Lynn Bresler
Illustrator Peter Dennis

Reading Consultant
Cliff Moon, M.Ed.

Research Source
Jamestown–Yorktown Foundation,
Virginia

Published in Great Britain by
Dorling Kindersley Limited
9 Henrietta Street
London WC2E 8PS

2 4 6 8 10 9 7 5 3 1

Copyright © 2000 Dorling Kindersley Limited, London

A CIP catalogue record for this book is
available from the British Library.

ISBN 0-7513-2931-2

Colour reproduction by Colourscan, Singapore
Printed and bound in China by L Rex

The publisher would like to thank the following for their kind
permission to reproduce their photographs:
Key: t=top, a=above, b=below, l=left, r=right, c=centre
Bridgeman Art Library: Private Collection 2 t, 32 tl, Science
Museum, London 32 cl; **J. Allan Cash Ltd.:** 31; **Corbis:** Bettmann
3, 32 cr, Peter Harholdt 10, Richard T. Nowitz 33, Tim Wright
25 b; **Dorling Kindersley Picture Library:** 2 c, 21 t; **Fine Art
Photographic Library Ltd.:** Private Collection 28; **Jamestown-
Yorktown Foundation:** 7 b, 32 bl; **Borough Council of King's
Lynn and West Norfolk:** 2 b, 32 br; **Paul Weston:** 5 b.

see our complete
catalogue at

www.dk.com

DORLING KINDERSLEY *READERS*

BEGINNING 2 TO READ ALONE

The Story of
Pocahontas

Written by Caryn Jenner

A Dorling Kindersley Book

"I have seen pale strangers!"
A hunter returned
to the Indian village
shouting the news.
"They are building a town."

Pocahontas ran to listen.
"Isn't it exciting, Father?"
said Pocahontas.
Her father, Chief Powhatan,
frowned, "We shall see."

A long journey
The first settlers took five months to sail from England to America. They arrived in April 1607.

Powhatan sent Pocahontas
and a group of scouts
to the strangers' town.
They walked silently,
hiding among the trees.
Everything about the settlers
was strange.
Some even had hair on their faces!

Bravely, Pocahontas stepped forward and greeted them with a smile. A hairy-faced man smiled back.

The new land

The settlers unloaded their ships and set off to explore America. They hoped to find gold and other riches.

Pocahontas made many visits
to the settlers' town.
She learned that the smiling man
with the hairy face
was Captain John Smith.
The settlers were from England.
They called their new home
Jamestown, after their ruler,
King James.

Sometimes Pocahontas brought
food for the hungry settlers.
They knew many things but
they did not know
how to grow corn.

Pocahontas liked the settlers but
many other Indians did not.
Chief Powhatan held a meeting.
"The pale strangers mean trouble,"
he told his people.
"If we attack them, they will go away."
"Father, let's be friends with them,"
said Pocahontas.
"Strangers take our land,"
said Powhatan.
"They cannot be trusted."

Chief Powhatan
Pocahontas's father,
Powhatan, was chief
of more than 14,000
Indians. His tribes lived
in many nearby villages.

11

Powhatan's warriors took
Captain Smith as a prisoner.

"Let him go, Father,"
Pocahontas pleaded.
"No," said Powhatan.
"We must show the strangers
that there are a great many of us.
Then they will not fight us."

The warriors took Captain Smith
to see many Indian villages.
The Indians treated him well but
they would not let him go free.

One day, Powhatan held a feast
in his own village.
Pocahontas watched as the warriors
arrived with Captain Smith.
Powhatan gave a signal.
Suddenly, the warriors
swung their clubs over Smith's head.

Pocahontas raced forward.

"Stop!" she shouted.

"Don't kill him!"

Powhatan ordered the warriors
to put down their clubs.

"You are lucky," he told Smith.

"My daughter has saved your life."

Pocahontas and John Smith
became friends.
Smith taught Pocahontas
to speak English and
she taught him some Indian words.
Pocahontas asked her father
to help the settlers as
they were not used
to the harsh winter.

Chief Powhatan gave them food
from the autumn harvest.
The settlers were grateful and,
for a while, the Indians and
settlers lived in peace.

One day, another ship arrived,
bringing more English settlers.
The new settlers took more land.
This made Powhatan angry but
Pocahontas and Captain Smith
tried to keep the peace.
But the Indians and the settlers
did not like each other.

Winter came again.
Captain Smith wanted to trade
English goods for food.
He camped near
Powhatan's village.

Pocahontas heard her father
planning to attack the camp.

Pocahontas waited
until everyone was asleep.
Then she walked
through the wind and snow
to warn her friend.
"You have saved me again,
Pocahontas," said Smith.

Many seasons passed.
Pocahontas grew into
a young woman and
moved to a new village.
She heard that her friend,
John Smith, had died.
The Indians and settlers
continued to fight.

One day, an English ship
docked near the village.
Pocahontas went on board to visit.
The ship's captain, Captain Argall,
would not let her leave.
She was kidnapped!

Captain Argall took Pocahontas
to a new town near Jamestown
where she learned to live
like a settler.
She wore heavy cloth dresses and
a cap on her head.

She went to church
with her new friends,
who baptized her and gave her
the English name Rebecca.

The settlers' church

Church was very important to the settlers, and Pocahontas was baptized into the Christian religion.

All the settlers liked Pocahontas,
especially a man named John Rolfe.
Pocahontas wanted to marry him.
Powhatan made peace
with the settlers to celebrate
his daughter's marriage.
It was the best wedding present
Pocahontas could have had.
Pocahontas and her husband
had a baby named Thomas.
Then they all sailed
across the ocean
to visit England.

"What do you think of England?"
John Rolfe asked his wife.
"There are so many people!"
Pocahontas replied.
The people stared at Pocahontas
because they had never seen
an Indian before.
She remembered
how she had stared
when she first saw the settlers.
So she just smiled.

A visit to England
In England, many people
wanted to meet
Pocahontas and
learn about America

King James and Queen Anne
thought Pocahontas was charming.

Pocahontas had been in England
for several months
when she became ill.
One day, she had a surprise visitor.

It was Captain Smith!

"You're alive!" gasped Pocahontas.

"Alive and well," Smith replied.

"And you must get well, too."

Sadly, Pocahontas did not get better.

She was only 21 years old

when she died.

Pocahontas helped to bring

peace and friendship between

the settlers and Indians in America.

A memorial

This statue stands in Gravesend, England, where Pocahontas was buried. She is remembered as a brave and clever girl.

Indians and Settlers

In 1492, Christopher Columbus set sail for India. He landed at America instead! But he called the Native Americans "Indians".

Pocahontas was about eleven years old when the settlers arrived in Jamestown in 1607. Pocahontas is a nickname which means "playful". Her real name was Matoaka.

When the Pilgrim Fathers heard about Jamestown, they decided to sail to America, too. Their ship, the *Mayflower*, landed in Plymouth, Massachusetts, in 1620.

Pocahontas's son, Thomas, grew up in England. As an adult, he returned to live in America on land given to him by his grandfather, Chief Powhatan.

You can visit a re-creation of Pocahontas's village and the Jamestown settlement near the original site in Virginia.